Deliver Us From Evil

The Prayer of Our Lord

JOHN B. COBURN

Photographs by Ray Ellis

Deliver Us From Evil

A CROSSROAD BOOK
THE SEABURY PRESS · NEW YORK

Deliver Us From Evil

The Prayer of Our Lord

JOHN B. COBURN

Photographs by Ray Ellis

The Seabury Press
815 Second Avenue
New York, N.Y. 10017

Original copyright © 1973 by John B. Coburn
This arrangement copyright © 1976 by The Seabury Press, Inc.
Printed in the United States of America

Library of Congress Catalog Card Number: 76-20198
ISBN: 0-8164-2124-2

LIVING AND PRAYING

How are we to live? How are we to pray? How are we to relate the two, living and praying, so that praying seems reasonable and intelligent, and living becomes more assured and more significant?

First of all the living. The living is your business. Nobody else can tell you how to live. You have to find out for yourself. You do so simply in the process of living so that you come sooner or later to adopt certain guidelines for your life. "This," you say, "is the way I want to live. Somebody else may do it differently but this is the way for me."

You have your life to live, and since it is the only life you have, it had better be lived pretty much, insofar as you can, on your terms. So let us examine some of the terms.

What are the terms that you lay down as absolutely indispensable? What do you absolutely have to have to live as you want to? Is it a decent job and a decent family? Is it money in the bank and a wife (or husband) who loves you? Is it to have a purpose in life so you have a sense that your life counts for something? What are your own guidelines for a satisfying life for yourself?

There are a few questions you can ask yourself. For example, what areas of your life are most important to you: Your family life?

Your professional life? Your sexual life? Your social life? Your community life?

What are the areas in your life where you feel you are just drifting pointlessly? Your marriage? Your family? Your work?

Where are the greatest demands laid upon you? What parts of your life do you have to deal with directly and positively, lest they get out of hand? Your drinking? Your busyness? Your having no time for anything or anybody except business? Your tendency to be obsessed by your work? What presses upon you so that you have to pay attention to it if you are to get on with living?

Where are you most fully alive? Where do you come together and live most completely as yourself? When you step into your office? When you come home at night? When you go to a party? When you create something with your hands? Where are you and what are you doing when you are most alive? Is it when you are glad just to be yourself?

We will return to these questions about living later. They are questions only you can answer. By the time we return, perhaps you will have formulated some answers of your own from out of your own life.

Now the praying—and we are going to turn directly to the Lord's Prayer and ask Jesus to do for us what his disciples asked him to do when they said, "Lord, teach us to pray."

How he answered that question is what we are concerned with here, for how he taught his disciples to pray may provide us with a key to our own praying and hence with our living. If we can catch something of the spirit with which he prayed, and which he conveyed to his disciples in his prayer, then perhaps in both our living and praying we may express something of his own authenticity—and thus become more authentic ourselves, living with deeper integrity.

There are two versions of the Lord's Prayer in the New Testament, one in St. Luke 11:2–4 and the other in St. Matthew 6:9–*13*. *We shall use the latter as translated in the Revised Standard Version:*

Pray then like this:

Our Father, who art in heaven,
Hallowed be thy name.
Thy kingdom come,
Thy will be done,
On earth as it is in heaven.
Give us this day our daily bread;
And forgive us our debts,
As we have forgiven our debtors;
And lead us not into temptation,
But deliver us from evil.

The relationship that Jesus had in mind between living and praying seems perfectly clear. In a very straightforward, direct way he says that in order to live fully you have to relate yourself to a power that is greater than you. You cannot go it alone.

Address that power, he says, as *you*. That *you* is best understood as a father, that is (in terms of Jesus' culture), the source of life, whose authority is unquestioned, and who takes care of the members of his family.

You honor him as you live in accordance with his will—or at least try to. When you are living as well as you can in response to him and call upon him to help you meet the demands life lays upon you, he will give you all the help you need. As you accept the people around you just as they are and forgive them as they do you injustices, you will discover that you also are accepted and are forgiven. Once you have that sense of being accepted by life, you experience the freedom to live up to your capabilities—to live fully as a person.

You have to remember, however, that you are only a person. You are not God. Your great temptation is to think and act as though you were. So you have to ask for and rely upon his help. As you depend upon him, you will be reminded who you are, and your proper limitations will be obvious. This will give you a proper humility and at the same time will enable you to be involved fully in the process of living—a process which you can completely trust because it is God's.

This is how prayer works to help people live. As an idea alone, it has no power. If taken merely as the description of a religious relationship, it may be interesting but will not bear fruit. As a prayer *lived*, as an idea put into action, however, it can mean everything. And only as it is lived can it mean anything.

So back now to the questions asked about your own living. What are the most important areas of your life? What are the issues of living that you cannot avoid, that demand your attention? Where do you come most fully alive? What are the questions you have to face in your own life if you are to be wholly yourself?

Perhaps answering these concrete questions as specifically as you can will be helpful: What do you want? What do you need? What do you long for? Whom do you long for? What do you have to have to live life the way you feel you ought to?

Those are the questions. Only you can answer them. What are your answers?

It is your life that is to be lived, and it can be lived only by you. Your prayer can be prayed only by you. How to put them together

—your living and praying? Where, in answering the questions, are you being pressed most to live most?

Take that "pressure point." Put it before God—any idea of God you may have. Perhaps you have only a hope that there is something greater at work within you, beyond you, somehow responsible for you, waiting to help you. That is enough to begin with, but preferably, says Christ, a God whom you can address as *you*.

Take, then, the "pressure point" of your life and incorporate it in the prayer of Christ.

You, here is where I need help. If I am to live fully, this situation is the one I have to deal with. I want—at my best, and this is what it is right now—to do what you want me to. I believe if I do, I'll be all right. Help me to accept this situation and all the people involved in it, and forgive them as I must. Let me trust you, and then I will trust what happens.

That is the Lord's Prayer *lived*. To live this prayer in your life is Jesus Christ praying. He is both living and praying in you. It is *his* prayer.

Pray it. He *is* the prayer. As you live it, you begin to live *him*. Living his prayer is to begin to live his life. This is the way to become increasingly yourself—and, in the process, increasingly his.

God—you—I want at my best to do what you want done, and I believe that as I do, nothing evil can ever finally happen to me. Help me to accept the demands life has placed upon me where I am and to accept everybody in it. Help me to forgive those I ought to. Let me trust you, and I will trust what happens to me. Now, and (hopefully) always. Amen.

THE QUEST
FOR IDENTITY

It is a truism—and one of the annoying things about truisms is that they are true—that most of us spend a good deal of our lives coming to understand who we are. At least it takes us through childhood, adolescence (rebellious or not) and young adulthood before we come to a clear inner conviction of who we are and stand on our own two feet on our own ground.

If we are fortunate, the unfolding of who we are continues through middle age into old age. New sides—unexpected sides—of the self appear as new relationships emerge, enriching different aspects of our personalities. It is not simply new work, new interests, new people who are a part of this unfolding process, but it is a new self, related to the former self or selves, which is constantly unfolding.

This self rises from within in response to the demands life lays upon it at every step of the way. It comes from the depths and brings with it memories, passions, regrets, hopes, dreams, convictions, disciplines, losses, failures, deaths, and accomplishments. The

more we are in touch with this emerging self, the more of a self we become. It is an unending process, this constant quest for our identity. It is the most exciting quest because it is what life is all about.

This consideration of the self leads us into the first phrase of the Lord's Prayer, *Our Father*. We know who we are when we know who our father is. We come to know who we are as we come to know who he is. It is a life-long process that continues to our dying day and then (who knows?) perhaps begins again on a deeper level of understanding.

The search for ourselves, biologically and psychologically, begins as we first become conscious of our relationship to others, primarily our mothers. It goes on so long as we are willing to pursue the quest and ends only when we give up spiritually, which is another form of death. We begin with an unclear understanding of those relationships; it is only as time goes by that we have clearer understandings, though life being the mystery it is, we are never able fully to comprehend the personhood of another.

Prayer begins for most of us in somewhat the same unclear way. We need help for living. We have no clear idea of where to turn for help except that it must come from beyond us. Whom we address or what we address in our cry for help, we are uncertain about. That is the origin of most prayer—primitive, confused, dependent. What such prayer grows into on maturity helps determine the maturity of a person's life.

Jesus said: However you begin as a child, when you mature as an adult you will address this power as a child addresses his father. You turn in faith and hope to a power whom you can trust, who wants for you a better life than you can imagine for yourself. Do not hesitate to lay your whole life before him and ask him for help. Say, *"Our Father."*

With the rising influence of the Women's Liberation Movement there are some people today who would say the way to address that power is, *Our Mother.* The comment has been made that a more proper translation for Genesis 1:27—"So God created man in his own image"—is, "So God created woman in her own image." Miss Pankhurst, to encourage a former generation of suffragettes when they were facing arrest, said, "Do not fear. Trust God. She will protect you."

These comments about the feminine quality of God are quoted for two reasons—the first rather obvious, the other perhaps more subtle.

The first reason is that the characteristics attributed to a father only, are not adequate to describe the characteristics of God. They point to one side of his nature but to one side alone—the side that represents power, authority, the "laying down of the law," judgment, reason, discipline. These are all characteristics of what we call a "father figure,"—the obvious symbol to use for God in a patriarchal society.

But together with the "father figure" there must be a "mother figure" for the complete representation of the characteristics of the Being who is the creator of all life. For the act of creation itself, a "mother figure" as well as a "father figure" is required. Just as masculine qualities are needed, so for the wholeness of life feminine qualities are needed also: the caring, accepting, nursing, nurturing, and feeding; the comforting, assuring, feeling, and intuitiveness—each of them grounded in nature and susceptible to its rhythms. All these feminine qualities are essential for life too, and in some mea-

sure and in differing proportions essential for every human being.

Both sets of qualities together point to wholeness in the ultimate reality of God. God is *all* life—all the created order—and more. So when we call upon him/her, we are calling upon a power who encompasses all that we know of as reality or that originally was borne in upon us by our fathers and mothers who brought us to birth —and of course infinitely more. Whether you call God *father* or *mother,* the limitation rises from our use of language, not from the Reality of God in his/her own Being.

The second reason why both father and mother relationships are necessary for our thinking about God is that we know God first and always through flesh and blood relationships. By extension, the whole fabric of interpersonal relationships, beginning with the family—brothers and sisters, uncles and aunts, grandparents and grandchildren, husbands and wives, parents and children—provide the matrix within which we come to our knowledge of God. It is indeed through these relationships that God makes himself known. The Christian concept of the Incarnation—God with us—is that he in Christ was made flesh and blood.

We came into life because a man and a woman had a personal relationship that included sexual union. It was through these parents that we were introduced to the fundamental relationship we were to have with the universe. It is they who fed us, clothed us, sheltered us, cared for us, dominated us, disciplined us, loved us, resented us, frightened us when they were angry, kissed us when they were sorry, punished us when we did what they considered wrong, and forgave our misdeeds, large and small. In their relationship to us they revealed to us the heights and depths of human existence.

Our response to them, and hence to life, as we were growing

up was similarly mixed. We both loved them and were frightened by them. We felt safe in their company at home, yet wanted to grow up and leave home—and to strike out from home we sometimes had to strike back at home. We wanted to accept them and to reject them, sometimes at the same time. We were fearful of their domination, and fearful of their death. We may even have envisioned their dying, yet at the same time knew somehow they would never die. (The relationship never dies. We deal with our parents until *we* die.)

These personal family relationships together with those arising from them and extending to friends, schoolmates and community associates—competitive, supporting, loving, hating, friendly, hostile—and our response to them determine primarily who we are, what kind of people we become. And when to God we say, *you,* we do so from the midst of these personal relationships.

We pray to God out of anger because of a father who has dominated us:

> *O God, my father has never liked me. He doesn't like me now. He never will like me. God,* you *help me.*

We pray out of a broken heart when someone we love dies:

> *O God, into your hands we commit him.* You *help him now. Help us.*

We pray out of a full heart when a child is born of the mystery of love and passion:

> *O God, a miracle. The gift of life. Thank* you.

[24]

When we are torn between loyalties, must make decisions and are at a loss to decide, it is out of perplexity that we pray:

God, what shall I do? How can I choose the best and count for the most? Make the way clear.

When we have deliberately and willfully done what we know we ought not to have and are overcome with remorse, we pray out of our guilt:

God, I am sorry. Forgive me. You *forgive me.*

The point is this: prayer rises from within the process and demands of living. It is through the pressures of living that God presses. Your response is through the living of those characteristics of life that you first came to know in those close personal relationships—through parents, family, friends. Your prayer is your response, and it is expressed in your living.

Consider questions such as these to help you identify where your prayer begins. How do you respond to authority? How do you respond—inside—to your superior in your office? To the person who makes decisions affecting your life without consulting you? Who makes up the rules of your life? Are they imposed on you by your wife? your husband? your peers? your company?—or do you make them up yourself?

Do you impose the rules on your children? Are you afraid to? don't know how to? don't care to? By whose rules does your wife (or husband) live? Do you judge yourself by the same rules you judge everybody else?

Who are the people in your life whom you comfort? When did you last comfort anybody? Who comforts you? Whom do you count on to standy by, be there, always ready to pick you up when you fall? Are you there for that person in the same way?

To whom are *you* loyal *always?* Why? Desire? Duty? Fear? Who is loyal to you always? Why? Because they love you, or are afraid of you, or are just trapped?

What fascinates you and frightens you at the same time? The thought of dying? An affair? A promotion? Going through psycho-analysis? Having someone you love analyzed? The birth of a child you are responsible for? Someone's death for which you hold yourself accountable?

What is there in your life that you sometimes think makes life unbearable? Why then do you bear it? Are there responsibilities you wish you did not have; but since you have to have them, you won't let them go? Why is that?

What are the relationships in your life that seem to have lost all meaning and no longer make sense? Why? What can you do about them? Break them? Embrace them? Cut them off or go deeper into them?

Where is the conflict in your life that must be solved and that you cannot solve? Where do you go for help? Will you face it? Repress it? What will you do?

Where—in a word—are the pressures of your life that are *forcing* you beyond yourself? That is God pressing. The One to whom when you pray you can say, *you.* You can live through those pressures to him because that is where he is. That is to pray.

As through your living and praying you come to know who God is, you come to know who you are. The more you go to him, the

more of you is revealed. In your response to him in your living and praying, there is a deeper and deeper self-unfolding. You are in him —as you are in life. So as you go through life you can say in response to him:

"I know who *I* am because I know who *he* is; and that I belong to him. I have been through enough in life to have at least this much conviction about who I am to stake my life on it. With God's help I will continue to grow in that knowledge. It is knowledge and love together—knowledge and love of my brothers and sisters, friends and relations, all those personal relationships where we are bound together."

When you pray, then, out of this network of personal relationships, you pray to a personal God, *Our Father, you*. Your response is to the absolute authority figure in the universe who is also the comforter, the creator of all life as well as yours, and the one who gives meaning to it.

There is one final word. When you pray, do not think that you are beginning a relationship with God. That has already begun. You do not have to build it. God began it and built it. He established it from the foundation of the world, and so far as you are aware of it, through your mother and your father, your brothers and your sisters, and through *every* relationship you continue to have.

He made that relationship perfectly clear when he sent his Son into the world that we might, says St. Paul, "receive adoption as sons" (Galatians 4:5).

This is true not just for Christian people, but for all people— good people, evil people, people who love Christ, people who hate

Christ, people who never heard of Christ, people who wonder about, long for, Christ.

It is the Christians who know this relationship God has with all men because they know who they are; and this they know because they know who their father is; and this they try to make clear to all people as they try to live as becomes the sons of God, as disciples of his Son, by living and praying together.

Our Father, you. You made us. You made us so that we are restless until we rest in you. To rest in you, accept then, we ask you, those pressures in life where it is obvious we need you. And help us. You are our father, and we know who we are because you sent your son, our brother, to live with us and to pray with us. In him we pray, then. Thank you. Amen.

LOVE AND JUSTICE

God's kingdom comes as love in personal relationships and justice in group relationships are established. The kingdom comes within an individual when Christ is recognized as king and his laws of love and justice are obeyed. They all belong together—Christ in the inner self, love in personal relationships, and justice between groups within the nation and between nations.

In the last chapter we considered how we come to ourselves, to know ourselves, to love ourselves from within the family structure. This structure never determines the quality of life for one of its members absolutely—there are too many variables which enter into the makeup of personality—but in general it can be said that a child brought up in a secure, loving family is more apt to be secure and loving as an adult than is a child brought up in a loveless, insecure home. Other factors influence his development, but fundamental to this development are his family relationships.

It is within these relationships, as we have seen, that the child first deals with God—that is, where he first becomes aware of himself, of himself in relationship to others and to the life and the universe to which they all belong. His total life experience—awareness of the people around him and of the spirit moving through them, his touching them and being in touch with that spirit, of responding to them and to their spirit—that total life experience is both comforting and terrifying. It seems to accept him and at the same time to put demands upon him. He senses that he belongs, and yet he feels a stranger. He moves into that world just as he is and realizes that he is meant to become more than he is.

He comes to both trust and mistrust this life experience—probably both at the same time. The more he learns to trust it, the more he moves into it with confidence in himself. If, however, he gets hurt too much, he learns to distrust it, begins to withdraw more from it and to trust himself less and less.

How the child deals with his total existence is how he deals with God—or at least it sets the pattern by which he deals with God. It also sets the framework within which God deals with him—through personal relationships. Sometimes the word "God" is used, perhaps more often not; but used or not, it is in these earliest relationships that the attitude of trust (or mistrust) toward life is developed. It is here that a sense of meaning and worth for one's own life evolves, here that one comes to make one's own decision in life and to have the moral courage to accept responsibility for them. The decisions he makes in later life tend to reflect the quality of life known first in family life.

So at the center of the network of personal relationships that go on all life long is the family. This network is where we conduct our negotiations with ourselves, with others, with life, with the universe, with God. Even though we are living presently in a society where the family structure is weakened and often fragmented, and where an individual in the course of a lifetime might belong to a number of different families (some in hostility to each other), the

importance of the family is not thereby invalidated. Indeed it may be all the more obvious. Where family relations are insecure, personal relations tend to be; and the lack of structure in family life may be the basic reason for the increasing rootlessness in American life, for suspicion and for the sense of alienation and mistrust of people, as well as mistrust of the established order.

God is, of course, more than personal relationships. He is the creator of nature, of life, and of as many universes as may be. But he is experienced through the personal relationships that are formed in the first instance through the family. It is out of those relationships that there is developed the disposition to come to know him, or not; to love him or hate him; to trust life or to mistrust it; to respect and love one's neighbors or to reject them; to have a regard and love for one's self or to scorn even that.

Now, family ties are held together by *love* alone. Nothing else in the long run holds a family together—not money or tradition or power or prestige.

All personal relationships are held together in the final analysis by mutual support and common concern. They may be expressed in respect, mutual forbearance, patience, and any number of other human virtues—but they are woven together by the consistent concern for the good of another which is love in action. And love is God in action.

When person-to-person relationships are no longer possible because there are too many people living in larger than family groupings, then love is expressed by justice. It has been called "love working at long range." The best example is the nation, though the principle is true for the life of any group larger than a personal one.

Relationships are held together by the law of the nation and by the power that enforces that law. As that law is concerned to express *justice* for the people of the nation, the nation will flourish (or at least survive); without justice, it will perish. The road of history is strewn with the records of nations that have not survived because of a failure to provide justice for all members of their societies. The power that lies behind "law and order" is the law of justice, and that is God's law. But "law and order" which supports the interests of special groups within a society only breeds violence.

This does not mean that all men are equal, but that all are to be treated with justice (just as members of a family are not equal, yet the family, when at its best, is one where all are treated with love). Nations rise and fall, but nationhood always goes on (just as families come and go but the family goes on generation after generation, culture after culture).

The aspiration that men of different nations have for one family of nations to be born is part of the eternal aspiration of mankind. This longing for nations to be united in one family where men know they belong to one another, not because they belong to a particular national family, but to the family of mankind, is a universal hope. It is a sign that springs from a common understanding that beneath all surface differences the family of man is one.

Therefore, when we pray, "thy kingdom come," we are asking for this rule to become more apparent in both our personal lives and in our national life, with love prevailing in the one and justice prevailing in the other. It is the same God attempting to establish his kingdom among men—through love in personal relationships and through justice within the nation and among the nations. The law

of love among persons and the law of justice among nations are the same law. It is that law which rules in his kingdom. And the signs are all around us.

The God of personal love and of social justice is the same God. We cannot pray to God to work in our personal lives without at the same time doing all we can to help him bring greater justice to our national life. To ask God to build one part of his kingdom in our personal lives and to ignore the other part in our national life is to make a mockery of the prayer, "thy kingdom come." God is one God. He comes all of a piece, and his kingdom is a single kingdom: a kingdom of love among people and of justice in nations.

God's kingdom is where he is king. We are in his kingdom fully when his rule prevails in both our personal and national lives. In neither case does it mean that we are perfect citizens. In both cases it means that we are trying to respond to his rule in such a way that we may become more loving in our personal relationships and, on the national scene, may achieve a more just social order for all persons. This means, as citizens, we take our civic and community responsibilities as seriously as we do our personal, family ones.

To pray, "thy kingdom come" is to declare that God is as concerned about quality education in all schools as you are about the choice of school for your children. It is to acknowledge that you have responsibilities as citizens as you do as parents.

To pray, "thy kingdom come" is to state that God is as involved in the voting of just abortion legislation as he is in your own love life—and that you have responsibilities in both.

To pray, "thy kingdom come" is to say that God cares as much for the writing of laws to close tax loopholes as he does about your own honesty in listing charitable deductions on your tax forms—and that you are as responsible for the one as for the other.

All life is a piece—personal and social, public and private—because God is one. When we ask him to come to establish his kingdom, he has to come altogether as sole king. He is where man is, where life is—personal and national—and that is where his kingdom is established.

When we pray "thy kingdom come," we pray for loving hearts and just laws; we pray for peace in our hearts, for peace in our land through justice for all men; and for peace through justice among the nations—the family of nations. The kingdom of peace is one kingdom.

It is not simply that the kingdom will come. The kingdom *has* come, for the king has come. It is now being established in your own inner life, in the life of your family and of your nation—in all families and all nations, with people knowing that they belong to one another.

So all we need do is to live as becomes men and women who already know their king and that he has come—in Jesus Christ our Lord.

Our Father, may your kingdom come
. . . in our hearts . . . in our families
. . . in our nation . . . among all nations
. . . in all men everywhere.
                              Amen.

DECISIONS
AND DISCIPLESHIP

The Lord's Prayer was taught by Jesus to his disciples when they asked him how to pray. The assumption of praying his prayer was discipleship.

When we question the validity of prayer because our prayers are not (or seem not to be) answered, it may be because we have forgotten this assumption of discipleship. A disciple follows his master. He recognizes his leader. He tries to do what his leader asks him to. He recognizes his guru, and when his guru speaks, he accepts the wisdom of his words.

When Jesus spoke about prayer he was definite, practical, affirmative, and positive. (The same cannot be said for all his sayings, some of which are highly paradoxical and enigmatic.) "Ask," he said, "and you will receive. Seek and you will find. Knock and the door will be opened."

When his disciples asked him how to pray, Jesus replied, "Pray *this* way." He was not vague, uncertain, or equivocal. "Pray this way: 'Our Father . . .' " So if you want to be a disciple, the way to begin is to decide that is how you want to live, and then to pray *this* way.

Discipleship has to do with decisions, making decisions in accordance with what your leader says, living the way he says to live. Discipleship is a sign that you have made a choice to live in a certain way. It is the setting of a direction to your life, the marking off of certain guidelines, the expression of a certain spirit. It is not just following a set of rules or of absolute principles, but the following of a person. A person will do different things at different times depending upon circumstances; but he will, if he is a mature person, bring to bear the same spirit at all times and under all circumstances as he makes his different decisions.

The mark of what it is to be a person is the ability to make decisions. To be made "in the image of God" is to be able to make choices, to make moral choices between right and wrong. This is the significant sign of personhood. This is not to say that the development of a central nervous system is not important in distinguishing man from animals, but rather that the qualitatively distinct human mark is the ability to distinguish between right and wrong, and to choose the one or the other (or more often one of several mixtures of right and wrong) in any given set of circumstances.

It is the choices we make that determine the kind of people we become. How the choices are made is as important at times as the choices themselves. The way children are helped to make choices as they grow up, for example, helps determine how mature they become. The goal of mature parents is to help their children come to make their own choices and to assume responsibility for these choices. Parents who deprive their children of making their own

choices for fear they will make mistakes deprive them of their birthright.

The mature person makes his own decisions and stands by them. An immature person may say of his decisions, "I didn't know what I was doing," or "Somebody else made me do it," or "I couldn't help myself." A mature person says, "I made the decision; I assume responsibility for it."

This is the first mark of what it means to be made in the image of God: *to make choices*. The second mark rises directly from it: *to live with the inevitability of conflict*. Human history without conflict is an impossibility. To wish we could live without conflict is to wish for Paradise on earth. That is a childish wish. We may remember Paradise, we may yearn for it, but we don't live there any more! We were sent out to live by making choices, and so history, the history of man and our own individual history, began.

Conflict arises because the choices that men make conflict. As each man develops, he makes choices that affirm himself: his wishes, his ego strengths, his will. His will never conforms with everybody else's will, because everybody else is making similar choices in accordance with his own will. The obvious result is conflict.

Consider this illustration. You are driving your car down a highway with your wife. Another car is on an adjacent road that merges into your road, and at the intersection there is a stop sign. The other car goes through the sign and smashes into your car.

You and the other driver get out. You say, "That was a stupid thing for you to do." He replies, "Don't talk to me like that or I'll hit you." He is bigger than you are, so you say, "Well, if it wasn't a stupid thing for you to do, it was the *wrong* thing. You went through a stop sign, and that is against the law. I'm going to call a policeman." You make an appeal now, not to his reason or to his good nature, but to the law, that power which enforces justice. The law has determined the difference between right and wrong, and you appeal to that which you are both obligated to obey. He responds, "Do that and I'll knock your head off."

Just then a police car drives by, stops, and the enforcer of the law gets out. He arrives "to lay down the law" and by his presence averts further conflict. He takes the license numbers, and you both drive off to meet another day in court where the conflict will be finally resolved. The law is given to preserve life, to reduce conflict, to help people make choices on grounds beyond self-interest and self-will.

The point of the story is simply to illustrate one dimension of the human predicament. Choices cannot help but generate conflict. Character is revealed in the choices a person makes. Conflict in this illustration could have been avoided in the first instance by obeying the law. We do not always obey the law; sometimes we take special delight in breaking the law, perhaps for no other reason than it is there.

Or, conflict once begun could have been avoided by your backing down and saying, "All right, it doesn't matter that you hit my car," even though your adversary has violated the law. For you to have done that, however, would have made you less than a man. You *should* "stand up for your rights" because what is at issue is not merely personal rights but right for all men. Justice must be done. So the appeal to the law and to the rights of all men is to see that justice is done.

Now when one car hits another car, that is one thing. But when one person hits another person, that is another thing. When cars get broken, that is one thing. When people get broken, that is quite a different matter.

It is one thing when one company competes with another company, and the conflict is resolved when money changes hands. It is something quite different when loyalties compete with loyalties, loves compete with loves, and people change—transformed for better or worse—because of conflicting loyalties and loves.

The crucial conflicts in life are not car conflicts, or business conflicts, or institutional conflicts, but moral conflicts. Moral conflict rises out of a conflict of loyalties, a conflict of loves.

It is very difficult—perhaps impossible—for example, for a son to be loyal to both his mother and his wife if both are competing for his love. If his mother will not let him go because of her possessive love, he will have to kill her—symbolically—if he is ever to become a mature, moral, responsible husband. That is *real* conflict. And it involves mother, son, and wife—all in conflict among one another and within themselves.

Again it is very difficult—perhaps impossible—for a son to become himself if his father insists on making decisions for him and on living his life over again through the son. Sooner or later the son will have to break away, go into a far country—at least symbolically—before he will be able to come to himself and become his own man. That involves conflict both between the father and the son and within each of them as well. But that is how growth takes place, growth in maturing, growth in self-understanding, growth in freedom in human relationships. Basic, fundamental moral conflict, in which everyone is involved in one way or another, is at the very core of human existence.

When we talk about loyalties and loves, we are talking about discipleship. Choices, conflicts, the resolution of conflicts that reflect our loyalties and loves—and sometimes, therefore, the creating of new conflict—is what life is about. This is what discipleship is about: making choices that reflect our loves and thereby enduring conflict creatively.

It is not easy to grow up, either as a person or a Christian. Growth almost always involves some kind of pain. The crisscross of competing loyalties and loves sometimes seems almost unbearable. To make choices and decisions involving competing, conflicting loyalties is the deepest moral conflict we ever face. It is the most painful and probably the most persistent conflict, and yet can be the most strengthening.

For the Christian disciple this growth-pain relationship was demonstrated on a cosmic scale in the conflict of Christ in holding fast his love of God despite the breaking of his body on the cross— a conflict that expressed God's mind as love poured out for mankind although it included the death of his Son. *Through* that breaking and death, the disciples came to sense a new power for living, a new strength they had not possessed before, a new life which they called a risen life with Christ.

That power is made available for disciples in their moral conflicts in every age. It is available today. Strength for living creatively arises out of conflict as people are faithful in their discipleship. Your moral conflicts, painful as they are, will be resolved as you remain faithful to your conflicting loves. He resolves them as surely today as once upon the cross. *He* brings the resolution.

To appropriate the power of Christ's action for your own living in conflict is quite simply to pray: "Lord, what do *you* want? What

[53]

do you expect? What do you want me to do?'' The question you ask is not, ''What do I want?'' but ''What, Lord, do *you* want?''

If what you want is what the Lord wants—or even if what you *want* to want is what the Lord wants—the conflict will (with pain) be resolved (with power). If the conflict is not resolved for the time being, the pain will be bearable; in time resolution will take place.

You will know what decision you must make, or, more properly, perhaps you will find the decision being made through you, with you participating in, rather than making, it. Either you go through the resolution of the conflict or you continue to hold the conflicting loyalties together until the resolution rises from your life itself.

When you are torn, then, with the deepest moral conflicts, when you are faced with decisions that *must* be made, ask:

> *Lord, why are you permitting this to happen? What are you trying to do to me? What is your intent in all this? What are you saying? What do you want? What is the decision that promises most life for most people? How can I best serve love? How can I best serve you? How can I best love you? How best be a disciple?*

Live your moral conflicts and pray them at the same time. They belong *absolutely* together.

> *Ask.* He will answer you.
> *Seek.* He will find you.
> *Knock.* He will open the door.

He is opening the door to a newer, deeper, more creative level of your living. He *is* that opening. So hold on to it, *and never give up*. To give up seems to be the only sin God cannot do anything about. Christian discipleship is most simply always beginning again.

Moral conflicts that arise out of your discipleship increase rather than diminish your strength for living. Cutting off moral conflict cuts your strength as a human being. Holding on to it in *him* resolves it finally in his way. And that is where life—for a disciple—most fully is. Here in him the partly living and partly loving becomes the more wholly living and loving.

Not very good disciples, Lord. But we are disciples; at least at our best we want to be. Here we are.

Here are our wills, our loves, our loyalties, our conflicts. Here are our compromises, our going to and fro, our giving way to pressures, our irresolution, our failures to be loyal to love.

All these we hold before you and offer them to you, in whom we pray our discipleship to you. We give that discipleship to you now and begin again to live it as we pray it–that is, as you live and pray it within us. You are our prayer and our choices are resolved in you.

Amen

SEXUALITY, DEATH, AND LOVE

Sigmund Freud maintained that the two central questions of life were—how do you deal with your sexuality, and how do you deal with your death?

Jesus Christ maintained that how you deal with your sexuality and death reveals how you deal with God, and thus with yourself. The key to that relationship, he said, is love which "binds everything together in perfect harmony" (Colossians 3:14).

This chapter is about your sexuality and your death as they relate to your praying, and about the love which may bind both together. The theme, which you can test on the basis of your own experiences in living, is as follows:

Within you there is a spirit pressing you toward living in unity with God. That unity is your ultimate destiny. When it is attained you will become your whole self. Life being what it is, an ongoing process which is never finally completed short of death, you constantly come closer to becoming that whole self as you continue to grow.

The bearer of that spirit is your body, which includes your central nervous system, your brain, your emotions, your flesh, your sexuality. It is this complex which draws you, sometimes drives you, toward other human beings, persons who have similar bodies and flesh and the same sexual drive. These persons also are bearers of the same spirit pressing them toward unity with God.

The spirit searching for spirit is the significance of sexuality. Men and women are bearers of the spirit to one another. As they touch one another their spirits touch. As their bodies find each other in union in love, their spirits find each other. They are, for the moment, one.

This is the spirit of the living God. Through these relationships, expressed in love as spirit meets spirit, the bearers of that spirit come to know who they are—his—and that he is drawing them to greater degrees of unity with him and with one another in that spirit. That is the spirit of love.

Love, therefore, is carried by sexuality, and sexuality is carried by love. (Love is, of course, carried in ways other than sexual just as sexuality is expressed in ways other than loving—but those are other themes.) It is when a person is loved and able to love that he knows most fully who he is. A person, loved and loving, is most himself, most free from fear, most outgoing, most at-one with living and with others. That spirit in him is a foretaste of what his ultimate existence and destiny shall be.

Put into capsule form, the theme goes something like this: Sexuality creates relationships between men and women. Sexuality refers to the total relatedness of a person toward other human beings. It has to do with the placing, the affirming, the creating, the touching, the offering of one's whole personhood to others. *There-*

fore it is always a part discriminating, choosing, selecting. It is always deciding how the relationships shall be established, maintained, fulfilled, denied. It is always disciplining and being disciplined. Sexuality is not, in a mature human being, indiscriminate. It is precisely the opposite, and therein lies both its pain and its power. (It is hard sometimes to say No, but sometimes this is the only way you can say Yes to your total sexuality.) To be a disciple of love is to be disciplined.

When the choice has been made and the relationship with another is a concerned, caring, compassionate one infused by the spirit of love, each person finds his spirit in touch with another spirit. That spirit is eternal. That spirit is the spirit of Christ which identifies the true nature of each person. *That* nature is not destroyed by death; indeed death may open the way to a fuller, freer life in that spirit.

This is our theme, but first two observations and then a question.

The first observation is this: Sexuality and death belong together; and they are best held together by love. They are two sides of the same experience. Sexuality establishes relationship; death breaks it. Sexuality means you find yourself through a relationship with another; death means you find yourself alone. Sexuality seems to promise everything; death seems to promise nothing. Just as there comes a knowledge of yourself when you "know" another sexually, so does there come a knowledge of yourself when there is no one you can relate to. This is especially true if it is love which has held together the relationship broken by death. Sexuality and death belong together. And they are held together best by love.

In the face of death we instinctively turn to one another. Where does comfort come from, if not from one another? Where else can strength to go on in life come from?

The gathering together of friends and families in a home after a funeral, for example, often brings a new sense of relatedness to one another and to life. The unconscious affirmation of belonging to one another and the celebration of living rising out of dying is not an uncommon experience. This is especially true where the people who gather are bound by a common love for the person who has died. Certain kinds of death are very life-affirming.

Sometimes death stabs sexuality awake. Death, or the threat of death, seems at times almost literally to throw people into one another's arms. One evening some years ago there was a sudden, mysterious and terrifying blackout in the Northeast because of power failure. Nine months later there was an abrupt rise in the birth rate in New York City. Sexual relatedness was the natural human response to darkness and the threat of death.

John Snow, in a book on contemporary marriage, has given another illustration of this relationship between sexuality, death, and making love.

> The funeral was in a small fishing village on the Rhode Island coast. It had been a good funeral: simple, brief, well read by the priest. The corpse, before it had become a corpse, had expressly forbidden astro-turf at the graveside. A friend threw a shovelful of dirt on the coffin as the priest said, "Ashes to ashes, dust to dust." There was plenty to eat and drink at the widow's summerhouse afterwards, where Tom and Ruth saw many old friends from college, and observed that even the widow seemed, somehow, to be quietly happy. For her marriage had been a good one, short as it turned out to be, and she felt no guilt. When Tom and Ruth left the house, they decided to go for a walk on

the beach before returning to Boston. It was a clear, brisk October afternoon, almost sunset, with a high surf left over from a recent storm. The wind was down, and the long grass at the top of the dunes was a reddish gold in the waning sunlight. They found a bleached dock piling tossed back from the sea, lying close to the rising of the dunes, and they sat on it. Three surf-casters, spaced evenly apart like birds on a wire, fished for bass in the incredibly white surf. Lures flashed for a moment in the sun as they traced their long arc over the surf into the dark sea. "I want to make love to you," he said.

"I want to make love to you, too," she replied. He took her hand, and they began to climb up the steep side of the dune toward the golden grass. . . .

[John Snow, *On Pilgrimage: Marriage in the 70's*
(New York: Seabury Press, 1971), pp. 125f.]

This interweaving of sexuality, love, and death is deeply embedded in the very heart of human experience. One of the earliest stories to come out of the primitive era of Jewish history is the love story of Isaac and Rebekah. It concludes, as all love stories should, with this happy ending: "Then Isaac brought her into the tent, and took Rebekah, and she became his wife; and he loved her." Then is added this comment, "So Isaac was comforted after his mother's death" (Genesis 24:67). How appropriate!

There is no answer to death except love. If you want to comfort someone who has been bereaved, all you can say is, "I love you." That is enough.

Love, then, is the response to death; death quickens love. Awareness of the end of life sometimes brings a new beginning to love, a deeper understanding of one another, a stronger commitment to each other. Sexuality and death belong to each and are held together in harmony best by love.

The second observation is this: When a person prays, he prays alone. He prays out of the fullness of his heart within. Those prayers are shaped by his relationships—indeed it is only out of those relationships that he can pray; but his presenting himself before God is by himself.

When you pray to God, you pray by yourself . . . *unless* it is God praying with you . . . *unless* it is his spirit (Christ) urging you to pray, tempting you to pray, prompting you to pray, himself praying . . . his spirit within you already uniting you with him. That is the same spirit of love which you know through your sexuality and your relationships to people. It is the same spirit which binds you in your prayer to him who is eternal love.

Dying, therefore—when you are most alone—is not the end of life. It is the fulfillment of life. When you are able to accept your death as life's fulfillment as well as its completion, then you are ready to embark upon a new adventure which in faith brings the hope that all your relationships will be fulfilled in love as they are meant to be.

There are the two observations, then. Sexuality, death, and love belong together. You are alone in God in the love borne to you by those who love you and whom you love; and if your human love is weak, his is eternal.

So now the question. Your answer to the question only you can provide, and it will therefore be the conclusion, *your* conclusion. It is a question designed to put into perspective the matters we have been discussing: of relationships established by love, or relationships sometimes disestablished because of love, of the spirit borne by our sexuality in human relationships (love relations and otherwise), of the breaking of all relationships by death, and of our standing alone in God, one with him in life and through death.

The question is this: If you knew that the hour of your death was tomorrow, how would you spend the next twenty-four hours?

> *Our Father we thank you now for everyone in our lives who has been a bearer of your spirit of love.*
>
> *We name them now before you and ask you to forgive us our trespasses against them and against your love.*
>
> *Help us to be in love in all our relationships.*
>
> *Before you alone and in you alone may we help you hold all things together in your son and his love which has overcome death forever.*
>
> *Amen*

ACKNOWLEDGING IMPERFECTIONS

We begin with a question: What is it in other people you cannot stand? What characteristics do they possess that irritate you beyond measure? What really gets you, gets under your skin, about their behavior?

Is it the arrogant person, the one who comes on so strong that he gives the impression of knowing it all? Is it the beligerent, self-assured, cocky person? Is it the suave, sophisticated, aloof, removed person who never gets involved with anybody or any enterprise—and thus never gets hurt? The voyeur of life's parade? Is it the irresponsible, moderately immoral, slightly amusing, partly cynical playboy? Or playgirl out for kicks? Is it the hard-working, conscientious, moral, virtuous (ask him or her), self-righteous pillar of the community or of the church?

In a word, what are the characteristics of another person that really burn you up? Whatever they are—and they can be anything—watch out, for they may be your own characteristics. We have the tendency to dislike in others characteristics we see in ourselves but try to keep hidden.

At least this is frequently the experience of many of us. We just do not like people who come into our lives to straighten us out. Undoubtedly it is because we want to straighten *them* out. The reason we do not like their laying down the law to us is that we want to lay it down to them. We know we have neither the right nor the wisdom to do that, so we repress the desire or try to. Yet when they show us the worst side of ourselves by their insufferable arrogance, we burn!

As an example from my own experience, during the years that I was involved in theological education, I served on an admissions committee interviewing prospective students who were considering going into the ministry. I would ask them, among other things, two questions: One, what is your greatest strength as a human being? Second, what is your greatest weakness? More often than not, the strength the person named was also identified as a source of his weakness, and frequently was so recognized by him.

"I am," a young man might say, "very patient with people. That is my greatest asset. My greatest weakness is that I have great difficulty standing up to people even when I know they are wrong."

Another would say, "I am a very efficient administrator and executive. If I am given an assignment to do I get it done. My greatest disability as a human being is that I can be pretty ruthless if people get in my way."

Still another comment, "I have a very deep, very personal relationship with God. He has called me into the ministry, and I have no doubt whatsoever about my vocation. My greatest failing is that I don't care very much what people think about my actions."

This human characteristic—the intertwining of strength and weakness in a person's character—is one of the elemental truths in

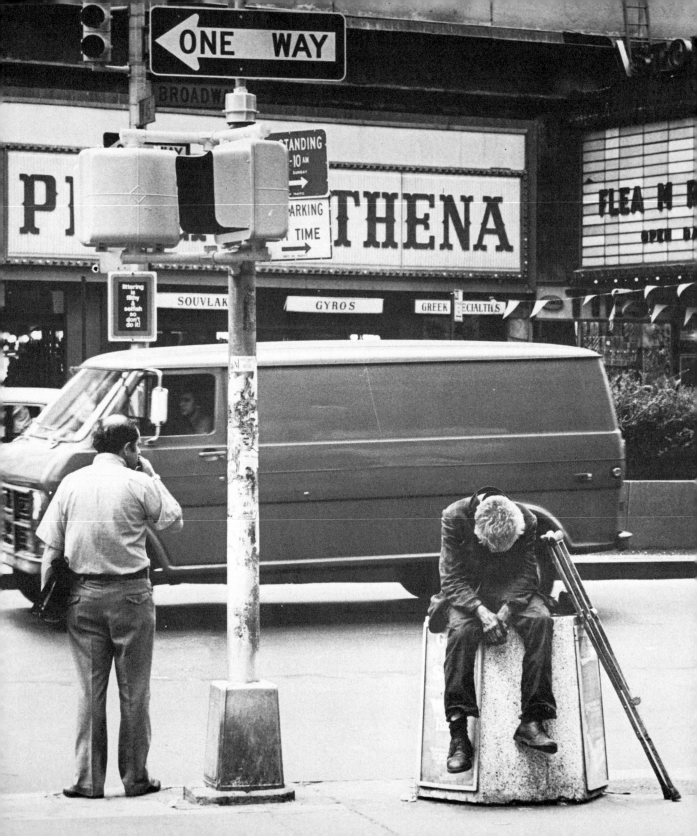

the history of men. The mark of human tragedy is that it is a man's greatness that brings about this downfall. When a man trusts absolutely in his gifts, those gifts cause him to topple. The myths of the Greeks acted out in their drama express this insight. Stories of the Old Testament, such as the Tower of Babel, tell it again and again. The classic tragedies of Shakespeare—indeed, the perceptions of everyone who has pondered deeply upon the mystery of human existence—describe man attempting to rise above his natural human condition, putting his trust in his ability to become something more than human, to control his own life, and then discovering (often too late) that he is not God, but man.

There is in man this curious mixture of greatness and weakness together, of nobility and depravity, of light and darkness, of love for another and of hate (sometimes for the same person). It is of no use to be told to "love one another," without recognizing the ambiguities and contradictions in love as in nearly all aspects of human living. What we love and what we hate, what we like to show and what we try to repress, what we consider our greatness and what we know to be our weakness—all are related to one another and interwoven in such a way that we are, most of us, a pretty complicated, sometimes conflicting, often ambivalent, always complex, never fully understood mystery.

So you are asked to begin with the question—what is it in other people that you cannot stand?—in order that you can consider the ambiguities and contradictions in your own living, especially in relationship to your praying, and in particular to that passage in the Lord's Prayer, "and lead us not into temptation."

What is the temptation? The temptation is to believe we are God. We think that we are God when we put ourselves at the center of life, expect other people to revolve around us, believe we can control our own destiny, sometimes the destiny of others. When that happens we are, in terms of personal relationships, asking for trouble; in theological terms, we are judged. We are judged by God. He alone is God. We are not gods. We may have no other gods but God —not even (especially not) ourselves.

The story in the Bible that sets the stage for the unfolding of this human drama is written in the third chapter of Genesis. The drama centers around the temptation. The temptation was brought by the serpent when he said to Adam: "You don't have to do what God wants you to do; you can do what *you* want to do. You don't have to pay attention to what God says about not eating the fruit of that tree of good and evil. If you eat that fruit and know good and evil, you shall be like God yourself."

Adam thinks to himself, "If I can be like God, I will be as powerful as God and do then whatever I want to do. I can then have free rein to express my gifts and exercise my will." So he ate the fruit.

When God sees what Adam has done, he says, "Well, man has become like one of us, knowing good and evil, but he is not God, he is man, created by me. He is mine. I am not his." So he sends him forth from the Garden of Paradise, and the drama of human greatness and human tragedy—man living—begins.

This story, like all myths, is not meant to be literally, factually true, but to reveal a deeper truth: the essential truth of what it is to be a man. And one of these essential truths, built right into the human condition, is that we are tempted. We are tempted to act as though we were God. But we are not God. We are men. And as men we ask God that we may be delivered from this temptation.

[76]

Therefore—and this is the point of this petition—let us acknowledge that we are men, not God. The best way to do this is to identify and acknowledge our imperfections. We need not pretend that we do not have them, or claim to be more than we are. To do so is to prepare for our downfall.

So, then, if in answer to the question, "What is it in other people you cannot stand?" you reply, "Their arrogance," look to your own arrogance. If you cannot stand self-righteous people, examine the reasons for your own self-righteous judgment. If you do not like to be straightened out, watch out how you straighten other people out. If you are horrified by the irresponsible, immoral conduct of young people, why do you protest so much? Whatever—whomever—you expel and rule out of life is hiding somewhere in the depths of your heart.

Lead us not, then, into the temptation of playing God with anyone; of judging people as though we had God's right to judge them; of playing games with people as though they existed for the purpose of giving us pleasure and satisfactions; of pretending that we are somebodies because we are so perfect.

We *are* somebodies—but not because of our perfection. We are somebodies because we are God's creation, his children. By ourselves we are that curious mixture of strength and weakness, of greatness and nothingness, of good and of evil. We must recognize these facts in order to begin to take on more fully God's nature.

The way to begin is by acknowledging our imperfections. You may recall that when Pogo was sent out into no-man's land to search out the enemy, he finally reported back to his commanding officer, "We have found the enemy, and they are us."

The enemy—that which we cannot stand in anybody else—is

us. It is part of us, part of our nature. To recognize it and accept it as part of our true self is to begin to put on God's nature. That is, we trust him to do what we cannot do: love the enemy, turn the enemy into a friend, transform him. *He* is transformed as we are transformed. In other words, little by little, bit by bit, we have to put on love.

That which you do not like to see in your nature is nevertheless part of your nature. The arrogance, for example, that you do not like, is, nevertheless, your very own. It does not belong to anybody else. It is yours. Can you acknowledge it? Can you accept it as part of your *whole* self? This acknowledgment and acceptance begin to turn your enemy into a friend.

When you have dreams that frighten you, remember that no one is having that dream but you. It is your very own nightmare, and whatever appears there, whether a snarling wild animal, a terrifying fall, or an embarrassing situation with which you are unable to cope, it is part of you. So welcome the characters of your dreams. They are appearing there to help you recognize yourself more fully so that you can become more whole. If you befriend demons they tend to turn into angels—that is, to strengthen you.

To love the enemy is to acknowledge, accept, and begin to love our total nature, ourselves. This is God's nature, enabling us to do so. This is what he does. This is God at work within us in Christ. We do not have to do it. We cannot do it. Christ can do it, for this is what he came to do.

All we can do—all we have to do—is to offer ourselves, our contradictory, ambiguous, divided, bruised, broken, very imperfect selves to be part of the nature of Christ within that he may make us whole. We do not have to resolve to become perfect, or even strive to straighten ourselves out. That is God's business. For us to do it is to play God.

We pray to be delivered from that temptation—the temptation to think we are God. The way not to be led into that temptation is to trust God to do that which he promises to do: to remake us in the likeness of his Son. That is what God sent his Son to do.

Let us trust him to do it.

Our Father, help us to recognize and acknowledge our imperfections.

When we see them in others may we thank you for showing us our true self.

We offer them to you.

We trust you with them—and with us—in your Son, Jesus Christ.

Amen

DELIVER US FROM EVIL

To be delivered from evil is to be delivered from any force that prevents us from living fully, wholly, completely. It is to be delivered from death. That is our prayer.

To ask to be delivered from death may seem to be asking for something impossible. We all die. Everything created sooner or later withers, decays, returns to ashes and dust. So to make such a petition seems ludicrous.

The prayer would not, however, have been given by Jesus to his disciples, and thus to us, if he had not meant it to make some sense. Let us see, therefore, what sense we can make of it by trying to relate the elements in our life which inhibit our living fully with the elements in his life which led to his death; and then we shall see what the reality is in such prayer.

To do this we have to begin with an exercise of the imagination. The truth that lies behind the mystery of existence is often illumined as much by imagination and intuition as it is by reason—especially if the imagination and intuition are not irrational and are supported by faith.

[85]

Imagine that your life is best described as a parade. It begins somewhere, passes the reviewing stand at some point and finally disbands. Imagine that the parade passes along an avenue that is one hundred blocks long. Your life began somewhere around the first block, was pretty well formed by the time you reached the thirties. Since then you have marched along more or less in step with others and with yourself. Now you are in the fifties and passing the reviewing stand.

As you pass the stand, a question begins to form in your mind. Where is the procession going? Where are *you* going? Just what exactly is it you have in mind to accomplish before you disband? What goals do you have anyway? Are you pleased—as you look at the backs marching ahead of you—with the direction the parade, your life, seems to be taking? What do the prospects look like? Do you feel that the best is coming up and you are pretty excited about it, or that the best has already been?

Do you yearn for "the good old days" when life was just opening up and you felt as free as a bird, when you knew you were going to make it a real triumphal procession? Do you wish you were back somewhere in the twenties or thirties and could start all over again?

As you look up the avenue—twenty or thirty blocks yet to go—do you feel up to marching them? Do the blocks look longer and longer, so long that you wonder if you will ever make it to the end? Or do they tantalize and beckon you, promising life even more exciting and significant than it has yet been?

What do you look forward to when the parade is over and you disband in the eighties? Do you think you will stop in at the first neighborhood bar you come to and have a cold, refreshing beer with your friends? (How many beers? How many is too many?) Or do you think when it is all over you will just go home, pour yourself a martini—how many?—have dinner, and then plant yourself before the tube for the rest of the evening, the rest of life? Or do you anticipate most of all getting together with all the people you have loved most and being content just to be with them and then together doing whatever naturally, freely comes to mind?

So, the question is, do you like what you see ahead? Do you see anything ahead? What, if anything, do you feel developing within you? In a word, where are you going?

Now as you ponder this question while (still in your imagination) you march by the reviewing stand, consider three reflections about the parade you are in.

The first reflection is this: Nobody ever asked you whether you wanted to join the parade. You did not volunteer for it. You never had any choice. You simply, suddenly one day found yourself in it, almost as though you had been shoved into it.

You will not be consulted about ending it either—not about how you will end it or when (unless you decide to commit suicide, which raises the question whether you decide or the decision is made by forces within you that you can no longer control). The time and place for the disbanding of the parade is not a matter of your free choice.

It is curious that we join the procession, and likewise usually leave it without our willing to do so; yet the procession is all we have.

The second reflection is this: Not only does a great deal of life —all life in fact—go on without our willing it, but much of it goes on *against* our wishes. We learn early on that we just are not going to be able to get our way all the time. "Life," it has been said, "is what happens to us when we're making other plans." As we grow older we discover that this crossing of wills, this conflict, is at the very heart of life, the character of life itself.

Furthermore, we come to see that the deepest conflicts, the most painful ones, are our own inner conflicts because they are conflicts of loves. They provide the central struggle in life. Then we discover, if we are fortunate, that often it is the bearing of those conflicts that makes life mean most (perhaps mean anything); that the bearing of them with grace, and if possible with humor, is the mark of the mature, growing human being.

Finally, we realize that the resolution of our conflicts is not so often something that we do to resolve them, but is simply what happens to us. The resolution of them comes precisely because we cannot get our way. *Life gets its way with us.*

So . . . you have to settle for a little dying sometimes. You do if you are going to live. You have to be willing, at least from time to time, to die to getting your own way.

That is the only way, for example, that a marriage ever works: a husband and wife both willing to die in some measure to their self-will. Without that kind of dying there is no life in marriage. The marriage dies.

When a friendship dies the only way it can be restored is for someone to say, "I am sorry." That takes some dying to pride, to insisting upon being right all the time, to any illusion of being perfect. But once that dying takes place, reconciliation can take place, and friendship can be renewed, even enriched.

This is how most relationships are retrieved from death to life. Parents sometimes recapture children who have broken away by confessing that they now have died to any idea that they were ideal parents who always knew what was right. To make that clear to your child is a humbling experience.

Sometimes the only way to make life possible is to die to pride, to insisting upon getting your way, to any illusion that you are so much better than another. Maybe the fact that life goes on so often *against* our wills is its saving grace—the fact that saves us!

And the third reflection: there is a curious relationship between the fear of living and the fear of dying. Coming to terms with life depends so often apparently upon coming to terms with death. Once we have accepted death—our death—the freer, it seems, we become to live. If we cannot accept death if is hard to live.

It is hard to love. A young man says, "I'm afraid to let myself fall in love for this girl. If I did I'd lose control of my own life and that would kill me." He is dead right! He *would*. That is the way love is. You have to be willing to let yourself go; you have to be willing to lose control over your own life; you have to be willing to trust love. Not only is that the way love is; that is the way life is. You have to trust it—all of it, including its ending.

Acceptance of death makes it more possible to accept life—the good and the evil, the conflicts, the defeats as well as the victories. This is trusting the whole parade, everything and everyone in it, and therefore taking one's place in it with confidence and hope. It means marching toward the goal where disbanding may not mean the end of life but its fulfillment.

In our best moments, when we have really sacrificed ourselves for another and done so gladly, we know that the parade is worth every effort, and we are happy to be a part of it. We experience our greatest power for living when we are willing *not* to get our own way because we love another. That sacrificing love is called atoning love. That is what life is all about.

The key to that life we see in Christ's death. It was a death prompted by love so that men might live. There is in that death, once we have experienced anything like it in ourselves, a power which speaks for itself. When we are in touch with Christ's death, whenever we live it, however inadequately, we are in touch with an ultimate power which is the reality embedded at the heart of the universe, shown by Christ in his dying which brings life.

The cross is the symbol of all this. It is at the heart of living because it has embraced dying. It points beyond itself to a new life, a new heaven, a new earth, for on it is the One who was placed there at the end of his pilgrimage for insisting not upon his own way but God's. So, obedient to love, from that cross he reigns forever.

When we pray, then, "deliver us from evil," we pray simply that in him we may be delivered from death and so not be afraid to live in love. Our living that prayer helps us become him: he *is* our prayer.

We have, then, *already* been delivered from death. We have been delivered from all fear of death in him. He has destroyed death by his atoning love. That is what the procession, the pilgrimage, the parade is all about. So may we live it just as fully, freely as we can in him who taught us to pray, *Our Father . . . deliver us from evil.* Amen.

Our Father,
    We thank you
        for, having thrown us into life,
            guiding us in our lives;

        for presenting the ending
            as our fulfillment,
        and the beginning of a new life.

    We thank you
        for the experiences of living
            which make clear, even to us,
the way of the cross
the only way of life.

    We thank you
        for him in whom we live
        and who prays in us when
            we pray to you,

        and who, having delivered
        us from evil in his death,
        lives again in our living
        in this world
        and in the world to come.
                Amen